Hawaiian Luau

FOR CHILDREN

By Robin Gillette

The magic of the Islands awaits
you, everyone loves a luau

Published by Vendera Publishing
www.venderapublishing.com

ISBN: 978-1-936307-14-2

Below are the names of the people featured in this book:

Brittney Keiper
Lannah Roberts
Lauragrace Roberts
Krista Hasty
James Gillette
Rocco Gillette
Zephen Rigby

Let's Party, Here's How is specifically designed to help you make that special occasion outstanding with decorations, fun food ideas, recipes, activities and games.

You may want to create a surprise party for your child on his/her special day. Or you may want to use the occasion to spend some quality time with your child in having him/her work with you in putting the party together.

However you decide to craft your party, these "how to help ideas," will guide you in creating an easy and exciting event. From our family to yours . . . enjoy!

Robin Gillette
"Let's Party, Here's How" Inc.

History

The Luau is a Hawaiian feast. In ancient Hawaii the people were forbidden by their religion to eat certain delicacies or allow men and women to eat meals together. In 1819 King Kamehameha II abolished these traditional religious practices by ordering a feast where men and women could eat together. Thus ended the old Hawaiian taboos and the Luau, as we know it today, was born.

The traditional Luau feast was eaten on mats rolled out on the ground with a beautiful centerpiece made of ti leaves, ferns, and native flowers. The feast could go on for days.

Celebrate a touch of Hawaiian life on the Islands with a luau for family and friends, or as a party for young people.

Table of Contents

Have fun. Be creative and surprise your guests!

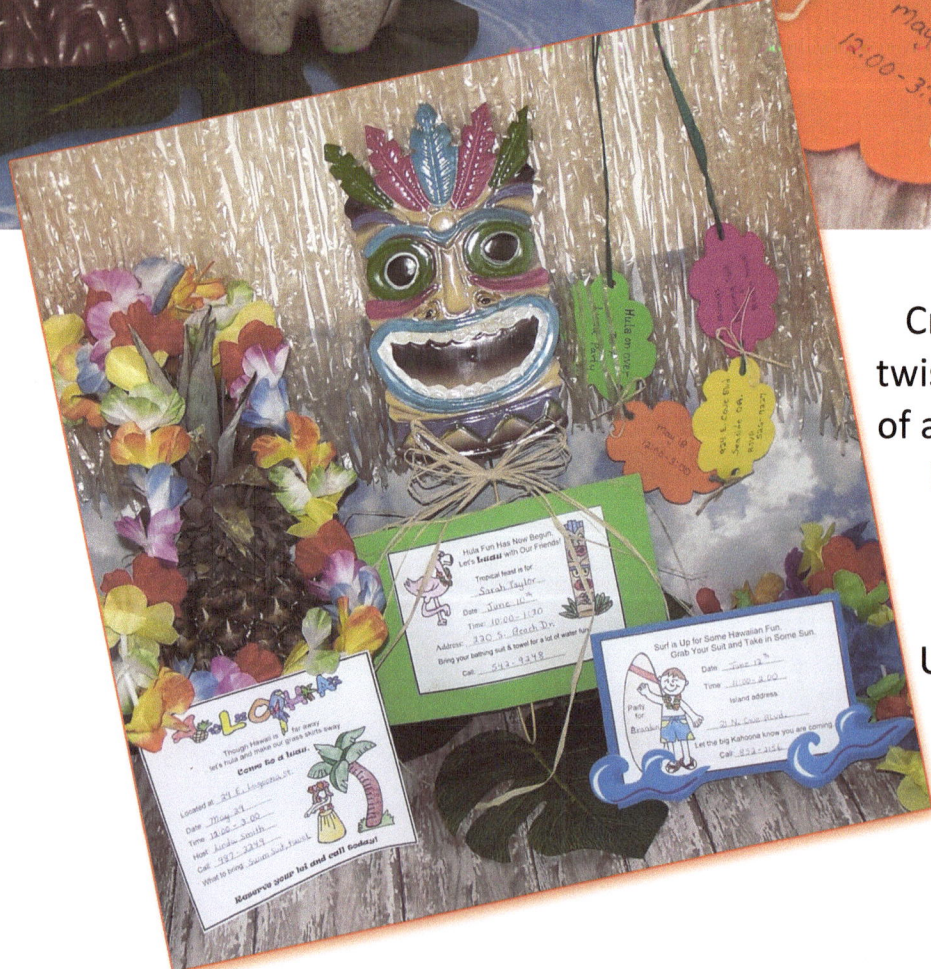

To: Sally Peterson

From: Sarah may

Hula on over To A Luau Party

Bring: Bathing Suit & Beach towel

may 18 12.00 - 3:00

924 E. Cove Blvd. Seaside OR. RSVP 526-9227

Create a lei invitation. Tape a twist tie, one on each top corner of an invitation and twist tie to a lei. Children may wear the invitation necklace style.

Use the following Ideas and patterns to design your own invitations

Invitations

Use the following patterns and ideas
to design your own invitations

f your child is helping you with his/her party, you will enjoy making these invitations together. Be sure to hand out or mail invitations two weeks prior to the scheduled date. Two days before the party be sure to call guests to confirm how many will be attending.

Floral Lei

Copy the flower pattern onto colored cardstock or trace onto craft foam sheets, four flowers for each invitation. Cut out the flowers. Punch a hole in the end of each flower. Use markers to write:

- On the first flower: "Hula on over to a Luau party ".
- On the second flower: Date and time.
- On the third flower: Address and phone number.
- On the fourth flower: What to bring.

Line up the flowers in the direction the invitation is to be read. Thread a length of green raffia through each flower as shown below. Tape raffia to the back to secure. Tie or tape the ends of the raffia together to form a necklace.

Note: For hard to find green raffia, purchase a green hula skirt and cut off strips. Using a child's skirt you will need two lengths per lei. Tape or tie the two strips together with scotch tape before threading through. Tie raffia bows between flowers.

Message in a Bottle

Copy and color invitation below, Make copies or scan into a computer and print out one per guest. Purchase small invitation bottles found in party stores, or use plastic soda bottles. Pour a little sand on the bottom of each bottle. Add small shells and glitter. Roll up invitation and place in each bottle. Leave a portion poking out of the top for guests to retrieve. Tie a strand of raffia around the bottle neck. These invitations will need to be handed-delivered, but Invitation bottles from party stores can be sent through the mail.

"X" marks the spot that leads the way,
to a tropical paradise where palm trees sway.
Follow the dots and you will see...
where the **party's** going to be!

Date: _____

Time: _____

What to bring:

_____

_____

Host:

_____

Exotic foods & lots of fun,
while swimming under
a tropical sun.

"X" Address of Luau

_____

Reserve your lei and call today! _____

Invitation Patterns:

There are two ways to make up the invitations:

1. Computer- Scan pattern and print out. Color print with colored pencils. Rescan and print number needed on colorful hibiscus flowered or Hawaiian theme bordered paper.

2. Photocopy- Photocopy number needed on Hawaiian theme paper and color. If your child is helping, have him/her color prints.

ALOHA

Though Hawaii may be far away
let's hula and make our grass skirts sway.

Come to a luau.

Located at: _____

Date: _____

Time: _____

Host/Hostess: _____

Call: _____

What to bring:_____

Reserve your lei and call today!

Hula Fun Has Now Begun,

Let's *Luau* with Our Friends!

Tropical Feast is for:

_____

Date: _____

Time: _____

Address: _____

_____

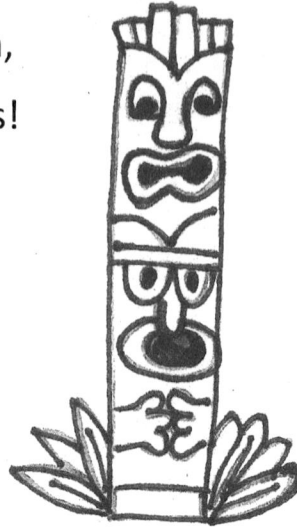

Bring your bathing suit & towel for lot's of water fun.

Call: _____

Surf is Up for Some Hawaiian Fun,
Grab Your Suit and Take in Some Sun.

Date: _____

Time: _____

Party
for:

_____

Island address:

_____

Let the big Kahoona know you are coming,

Call: _____

Guest Organizer

Call guests two days before the party
to confirm how many will be attending.

Name _____ Phone # _____

Name _____ Phone # _____

Name _____ Phone # _____

Name _____ Phone # _____

Name _____ Phone # _____

Name _____ Phone # _____

Name _____ Phone # _____

Name _____ Phone # _____

Name _____ Phone # _____

Name _____ Phone # _____

Name _____ Phone # _____

Name _____ Phone # _____

Name _____ Phone # _____

Name _____ Phone # _____

Name _____ Phone # _____

Name _____ Phone # _____

Name _____ Phone # _____

Decorating Ideas

Create a lush tropical atmosphere. Use a scented candle or air-freshener for that lingering island fragrance, and fans for a soft island breeze. Set the mood with CD's softly playing sounds of ocean waves hitting the beach with the call of sea gulls, or Hawaiian instrumental melodies. Purchase on the internet or wherever music items are sold

Decorating the Room

Below are a myriad of ideas on how to assemble an island atmosphere. Use your imagination and have fun. Turn your room into a jungle with real or cardboard palm and ficus trees.

To save money use artificial tropical flowers: orchids, bird-of-paradise, and hibiscus.

Take a small trash bag and place inside a small bucket/planter. Fill with dirt or sand. Drape the trash bag over the side to hide the pot. Arrange flowers in the pot and add greenery.

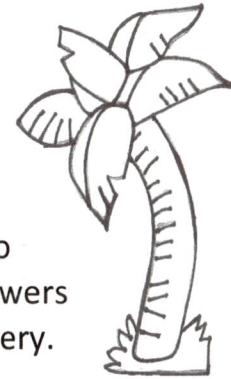

Create your own out of green construction paper.

Hang paper/cardboard parrots on palm trees or place on a wooden perch.

Use fishing line to hang a toy monkey from a palm tree. Make sure the object you tie the monkey to can hold the weight.

The totem pole is a simple cardboard fold-out. Attach to window or wall.

Tropical Paradise scene setter for backdrop. Available in many party stores.

Transform your walls into a tropical paradise using scene setter room rolls. The forty foot long roll can be used to decorate several rooms/areas, and there are a variety of scenes to choose from. Fasten the print above guest's heads and below the ceiling with heavy tape or a fastener that can hold secure during the party. Hardware stores carry several products that protect wallpaper and paint. Hide the bottom with brush, ferns, and artificial flowers in sand buckets, etc.

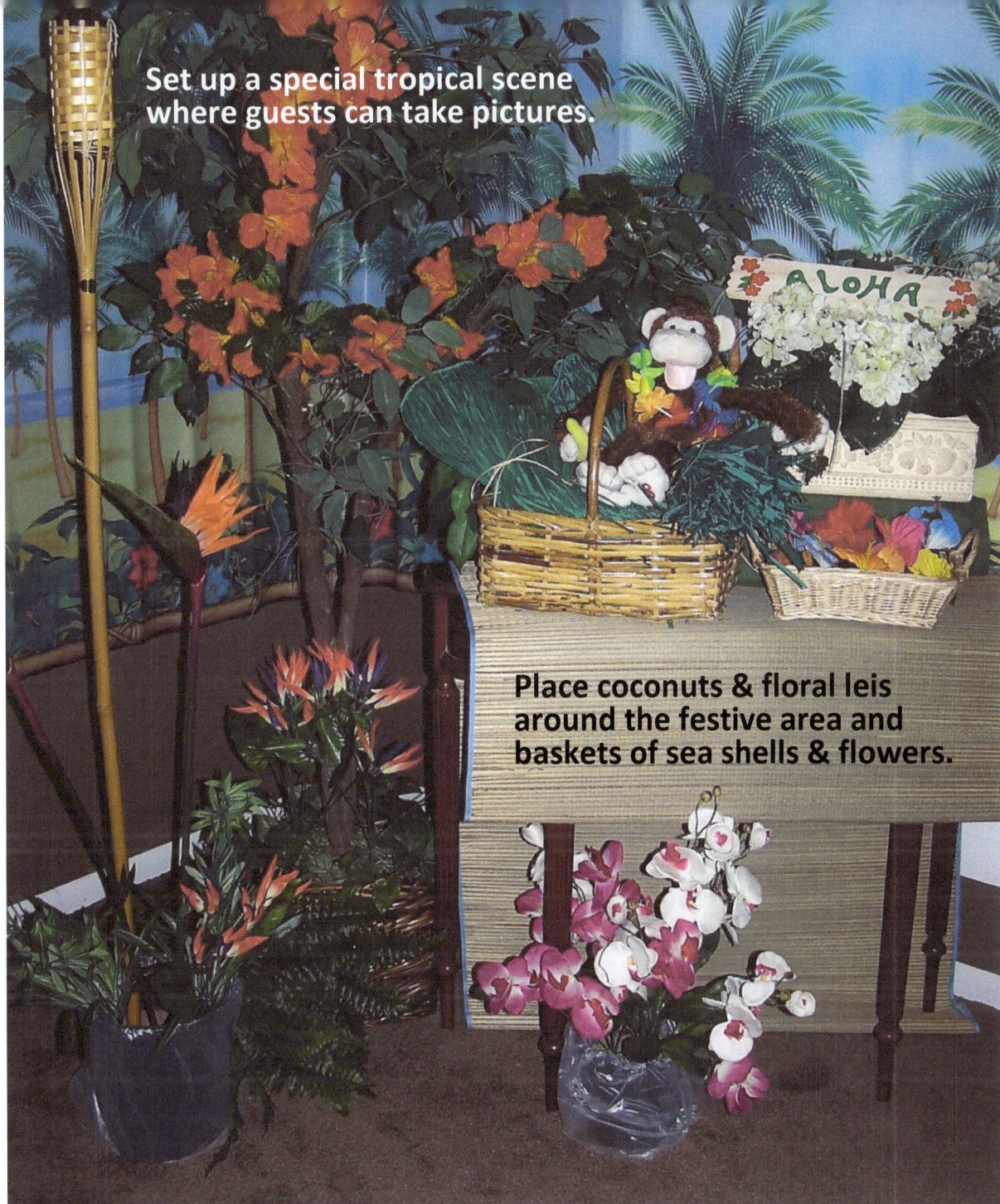

Set up a special tropical scene where guests can take pictures.

ALOHA

Place coconuts & floral leis around the festive area and baskets of sea shells & flowers.

Display artificial trees (your own or borrowed) around the room/rooms. For extra color, drape floral vines around tree branches. Cover tables with straw raffia or grass beach mats as pictured.

Indoor tiki torches pressed into buckets of sand with vines wrapped around the bottom are a great decoration but **they are never meant to be lit on fire!** Sturdy metal, outdoor tiki torches, firmly secured into the ground, are safe to light. Purchase fluid for torches before the party date. Keep paper decorations away from flame.

Tiki Snack Shack

A snack shack is a wonderfully refreshing treat on a hot tropical day.
Decorate with artificial tropical fruit in a bowl.

Shack can be used inside the house or outside on a porch or backyard.

How to Make a Tiki Shack

Materials needed:

- Two 4' wood tree stakes
- Ten 31" wood tree stakes
- Roll of black electrical tape
- 34" square piece of cardboard
- Card table
- Fishing line/large needle
- Two adult raffia hula skirts
- Raffia skirt for card table

Note: Purchase wood tree stakes at a hardware or lumber store where they will cut one 4' stake into two 31" stakes. Wrap electrical tape around stakes. Do not use packing tape.

Step 1. Place two 4' stakes side by side.

Step 2. Lay a 31" stake a few inches below the top and using electrical tape wrap around the ends several times to secure wood.

Step 3. Lay a 31" stake at bottom and secure around edges with electrical tape.

Step 4. Take two 31" stakes and place side by side.

Step 5. Lay a 31" stake across the top and secure with electrical tape.

Step 6. Lay a 31" stake across the bottom and secure with electrical tape.

Step 7. Have someone hold up the two pieces. Place and secure two 31" stakes across the top for support. Wrap tape around corners.

Step 8. For added support, secure two stakes, one on each side.

Slant top downward

Roof section of tiki hut needs to be lightweight. Use cardboard from an old packing box or pick up a used cardboard box from any store.

Step 9. Lay cardboard square on a flat surface. Draw a line across cardboard 6" from the top.

Step 10. Thread a large strand of fishing line. on a large needle. Lay the grass skirt down on the drawn line and poke needle from the back corner to front and tie a knot. Sew skirt waste to cardboard using large stitches.

Step 11. Lay grass skirt on top edge and sew to cardboard. Fold skirt edges under.

Sew the top middle stake to top of cardboard roof

Step 12. Secure cardboard square roof to structure with fishing line. Use the needle to thread through the cardboard and around the stake. Work your way across the top until secure.

Step 13. Wrap raffia skirt around the card table by tying fishing line around the top of the skirt and wrapping around the bottom stake. For middle and side sections, tie fishing line onto skirt from one end of table to the skirt from the other side.

Step 14. Cover table with straw mat or cloth. Decorate with tiki lamps, plants, etc.

Sew band to top of cardboard

Raffia skirts hang down from top

Create a Sign

Cut out a long rectangle out of cardboard. Using the grooves as a guideline draw and paint in the letters. When dry take several strands of raffia and twist together to form a long, smooth strand to be used as a sign border. Thread a needle with fishing line. Hold raffia against the edge as you insert the needle through the cardboard's edge, wrap it around the raffia, and tie a knot. Sew around the edge attaching the raffia as you pull the line over the raffia and pull through from under the cardboard. Allow extra to hang.

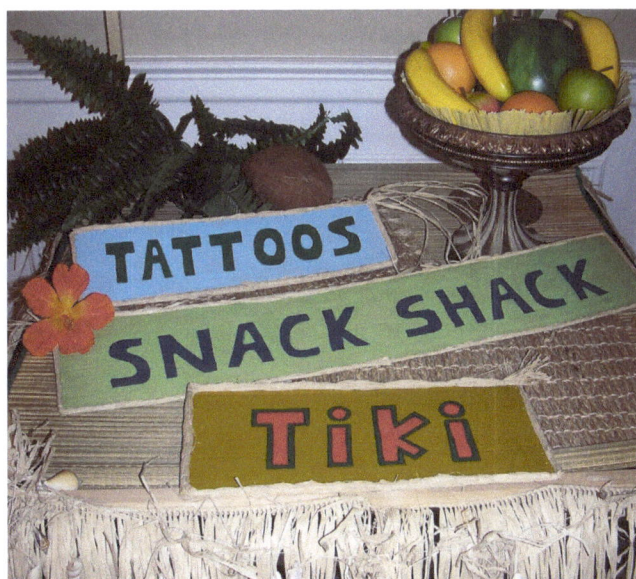

Does the Party Need a Parrot?

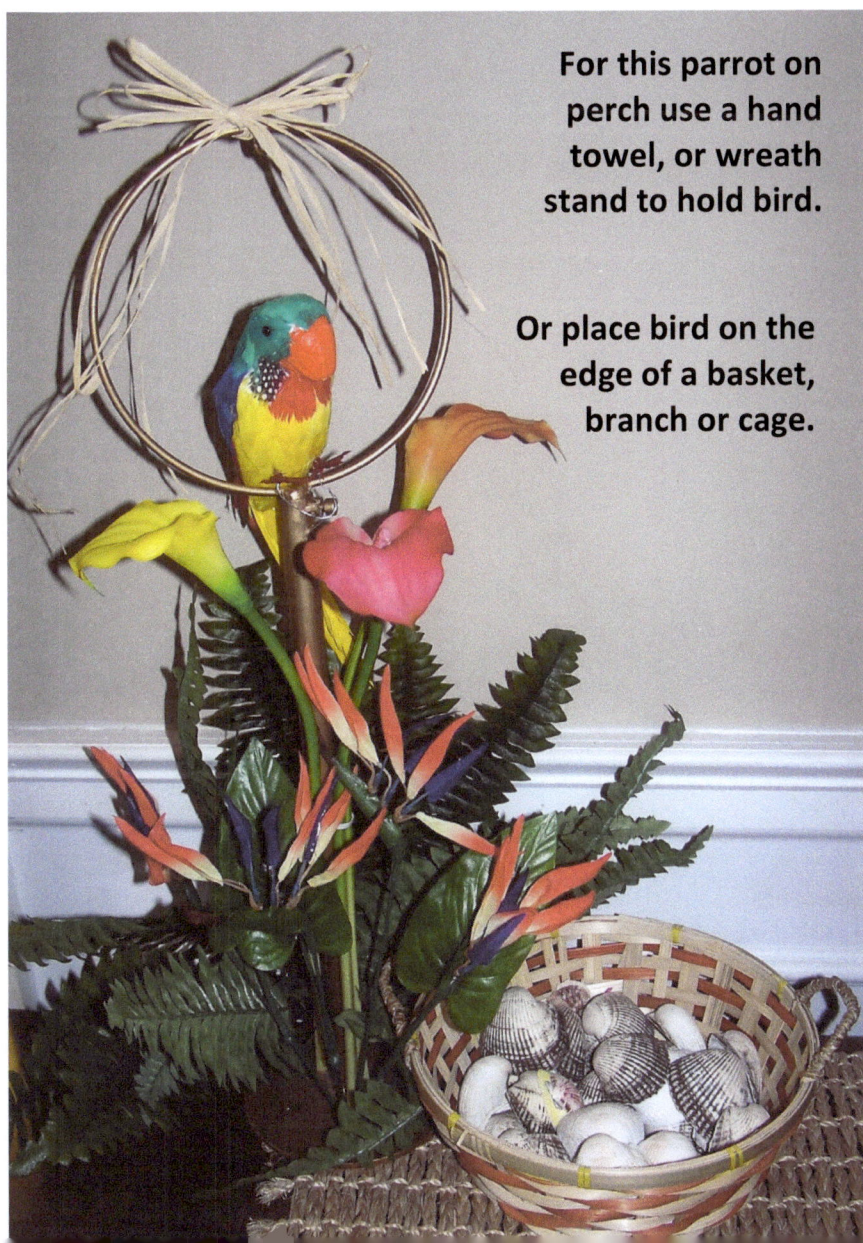

For this parrot on perch use a hand towel, or wreath stand to hold bird.

Or place bird on the edge of a basket, branch or cage.

Arrange flowers underneath the stand, hide the pole. Tie raffia bow on top.

Parrots or toucans are easy to find at any party store.

Exotic Outdoor Decor for the Yard and Pool

Hang colorful parrots from trees using fishing line.

Arrange artificial flowers in containers full of sand around pool.

Birds, colorful and mysterious, suspended from nearby trees or spied among the bushes add excitement to any scene. Some cardboard birds have movable wings that flap in the wind. Mix different kinds of birds together. Make scenes as realistic as possible.

Clear and invisible, fishing line makes an excellent cord to attach or hang any decoration.

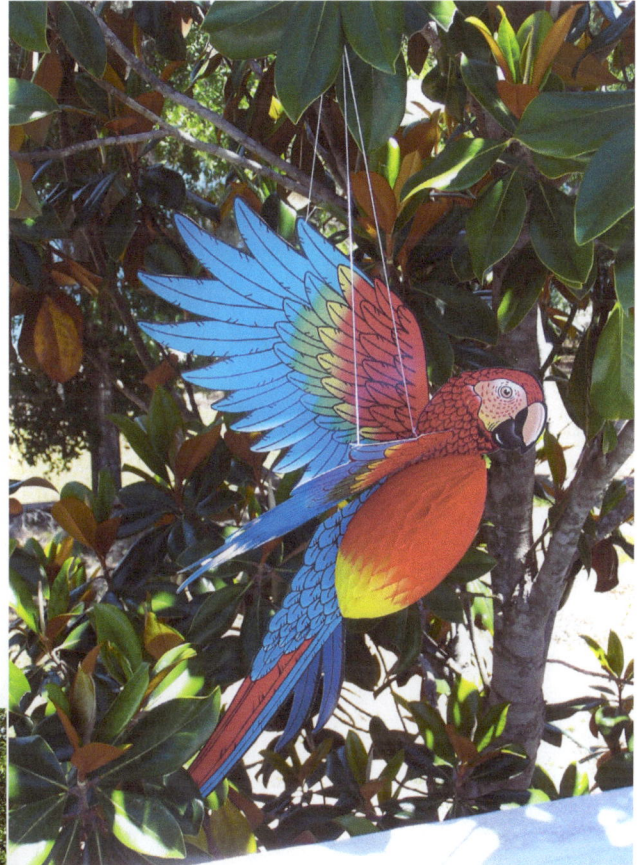

Arrange bamboo Polynesian tiki torches around the pool or back yard. If you are planning to light the torches, get sturdy metal stands that won't fall over. Do not use buckets of sand.

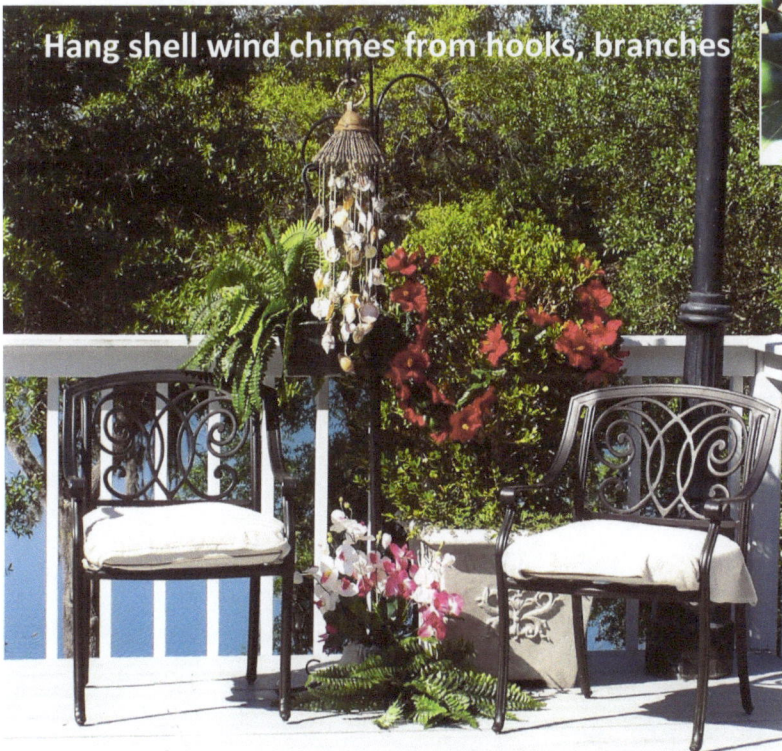

Hang shell wind chimes from hooks, branches

Create an atmosphere by using several small scenes with the same theme.

Arrange some areas in the shade for comfort and to prevent heat stroke.

Placing benches or chairs around the chime makes a great little nook to visit.

Arrange umbrellas in umbrella stands around the pool or yard for shade. Lay out straw beach mats for guests to lie on. Place sand bucket with flowers under each umbrella between the mats.

Drape flower garlands over small bushes.

Several stores now sell tiki umbrellas. Regular umbrellas will also work well if decorated with an island flair using flowers, vines, ferns or floral leis.

Tip: Keep sun block on hand to prevent sun burns and promote a great tan. Have drinks available to keep guests hydrated.

Under the Sea in 3-D

Attach an under-the-sea paper cut-out to a wall or fence. Drape a fish net over the scene and pull out the bottom. Secure with small stones, large shells, or drape net over a table. Attach fish to net.

Hang various sea animals from the ceiling with fishing line. Construct your own stand-up props. Tape paper or cardboard sea animals to small bottles of sand, use rocks, or any small, heavy item on hand. Add ferns for sea plants.

Arranging a Buffet Table

Set up one long table in the house or backyard. If near the pool, keep outside of splashing range. In serving buffet style, make sure children can easily reach the food items. For a large gathering, arrange food items on both sides of the table to form two serving lines. You may want to place cards in front of food items to identify the food. If you choose not to serve buffet style; set up a table for snacks, desserts and drinks

Go all out Hawaiian and have fun. Here are a few suggestions. Cover the table with bamboo or grass mats. Use tropical leaves and flowers to fashion an exotic table runner or centerpiece, or randomly scatter some around the table. Lay out coconut or shell bowls to hold tropical fruit salads or snack mixes. Serve Hawaiian bread in straw baskets. Spread tropical flowers and shells around the different serving dishes.

For serving table you will need one long table or two card tables next to each other.

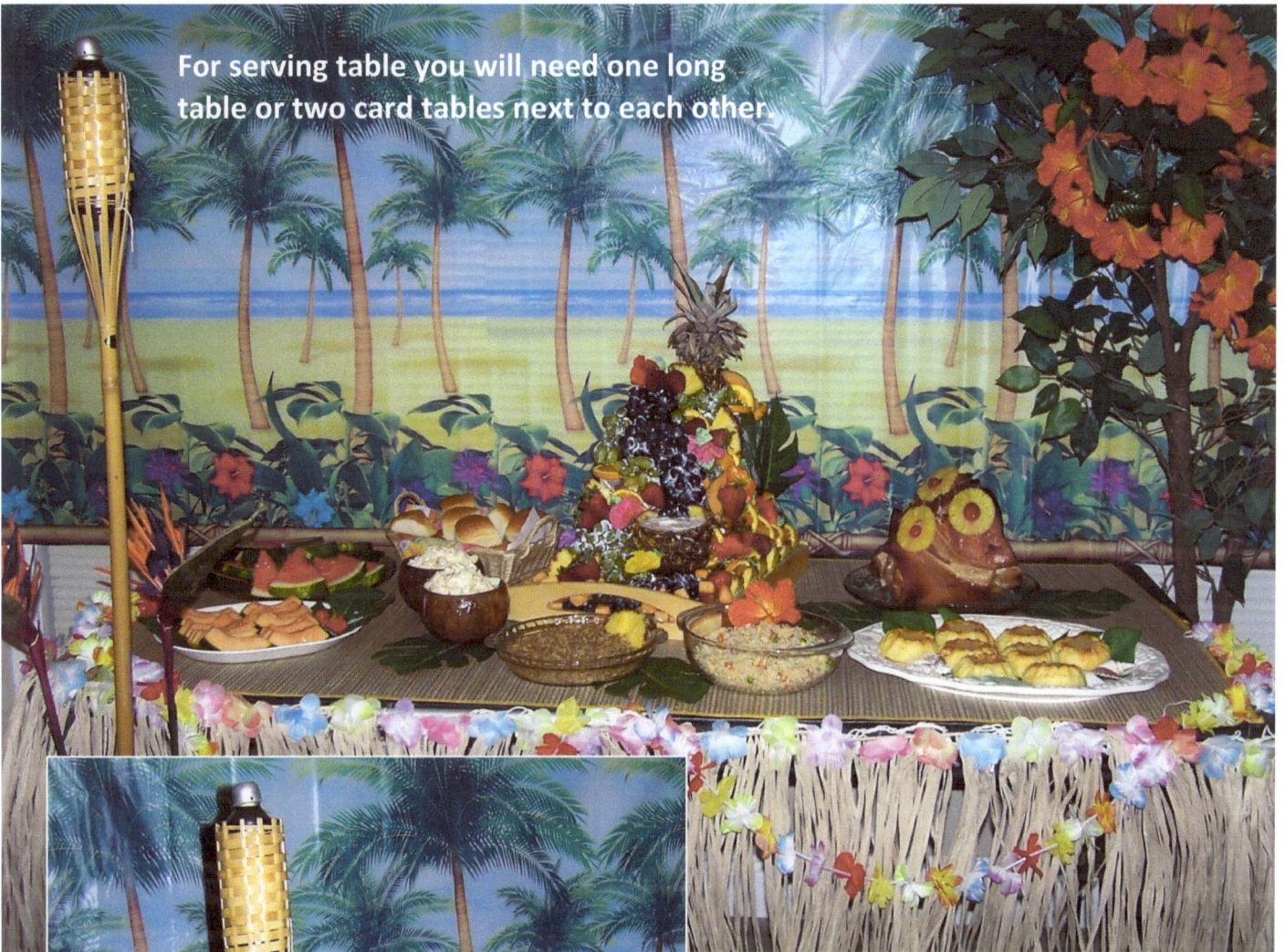

Wrap a raffia skirt around the table using table clips and lay a beach mat on top.

Drape garlands of flowers over the sides of the table. Embellish with tiki lamps, tribal masks and floral arrangements. Set plates, napkins and utensils at the beginning of the line

Table Settings and Decorations

According to Island tradition luau guests sit on straw mats laid out on the ground. Arrange several straw mats close to one another, children love to socialize. On a hot day place mats under an umbrella, in a shady spot, or on a covered patio area. Straw mats can be purchased from a party or department store in the pool or toy section.

Beach towels are great for children to lay out on the deck or grass and eat picnic style. List a beach towel as one of the items for children to bring. Have several on hand for those who forget.

Lay down a straw mat for each child. Use coconut shells for tropical snacks. If wind is heavy, place a rock on the end of each mat. Decorate with tropical flowers.

Use plastic pineapple or coconut drink containers.

Use a beach mat for a tablecloth and placemats for individual settings. Snacks served in a coconut shell set on top of a tropical leaf will add a touch of interest to any table. A hula girl filled with candy makes a fun favor or place card, and draped with a floral lei, it creates an added effect as well as something for a guest to wear. For amusement, garnish drinking straws with a flower.

Children are very susceptible to heat stroke. Be sure to keep guests properly covered with shade.

For a More Whimsical Look

Instead of using tropical flowers, you may want to fashion your own from brightly colored tissue paper. Lay several around the area, on tables, or tie some to tree branches.

Directions for flowers on page 64.

Flamingos are fanciful and exotic birds found in the tropics that can turn your table into something exquisite. Put together a flamingo centerpiece by inserting the legs of a flamingo into a piece of foam. Arrange tissue or artificial flowers around the base. Use flamingo party favors filled with candy. Fold napkins accordion style and fold. Add a flamingo straw as seen in picture.

Flamingo Favors

- Foam blocks (height 1 1/2", width 3", length 3")
- Wood skewers
- Pink cardstock paper
- Light green construction or scrapbook paper
- Silk flowers and leaves
- Craft glue/glue gun
- Small candy cup

Copy flamingo from the pattern page onto pink cardstock paper and cut out. Cut wood skewers in half for legs, one skewer per flamingo. Tape legs onto the back of flamingo. Cut 1 1/2" strip of construction/scrapbook paper. Wrap around foam base and secure with craft glue or glue gun. Have the paper ends meet in the back and hide with leaves. Glue leaves to the back of block. Glue candy cup to the top front of foam. Thrust legs of flamingo into back half of foam block and press flowers into foam around the cup. Write the names of guests on each favor (optional).

Hula Girl Favors

- Paper hula girls
- Colored pencils
- Clear small candy cup
- Scotch tape or glue

Copy hula girl onto white cardstock paper and color. Cut out hula girl and tape to candy cup or tape bands from pattern around cup. Bend arms on fold.

Arrival Activities

Listed below are arrival activities.

As guests arrive greet them by placing a floral lei around their neck while saying, "aloha" (ah-LOH-hah), which in Hawaiian means, "Greetings." Traditional Island music playing in the background will set the mood. Write guests names in Hawaiian on name tags and pin on each guest. Go to "alohafriends.com" to find English names translated into Hawaiian.

Here are a few Hawaiian words to enhance that Pacific Island ambiance.

- E komo mai, (eh-KOH-moh-mai), welcome.
- Mahalo, (MAH-hah-loh), thanks.
- A hui hou, (ah-HUI-hou), good-bye

Entry Way Basket

Have grass skirts in a basket near the entry way. Guests pick out a grass skirt to wear. Boys may prefer brown raffia instead of green.

Dressing For the Luau

Special Crafts/Activities

Set up several areas or tables with luau dress items for children to fashion their own unique luau costume. Choose a large area allowing children to move around with ease.

Activity Number 1 - Grass skirt with sea shells

Activity Number 2 - Flower headbands for girls

Activity Number 3 & 4 - Flower leis & bracelets

1. Grass Skirt With Sea Shell Belt

Materials needed:

* Grass skirts, one per guest
* Natural polished hemp
* Sea shells
* Plastic colored leis
* Small metal circles with holes (found in store jewelry section).

Preparation before party: Hot glue a small metal circle to the top of each shell to thread a string through. The jewelry section of a craft store is where to find a good selection.

Seat youngsters near the sea shells and let them choose a plastic lei from basket.

Note where the ends have been fused together and cut. On the side that is not fused, twist tightly and secure with scotch tape wrapped around the edge. Children cut 3 to 4 small pieces of string and tie the lei to the waist of skirt. Start from the middle and secure each end of grass skirt. Next children pick out 4 to 5 shells that have metal circles to thread the string through. Cut different lengths of string. Tie a shell to each string and tie around waistband of skirt. The shells should hang down at different levels What fun to see them sway when they hula.

2. Floral Headbands

Materials needed:

- Hot glue gun
- Glue sticks
- Various silk flowers in a basket
- Thin headbands (one per child)

Guests pick out a headband and one or two tropical items from the flower basket.

Have an adult or teen, hot glue flowers to headbands. Blow on glue to cool faster. When glue hardens children can wear the headbands during the party. The headbands are easy to put on and take off.

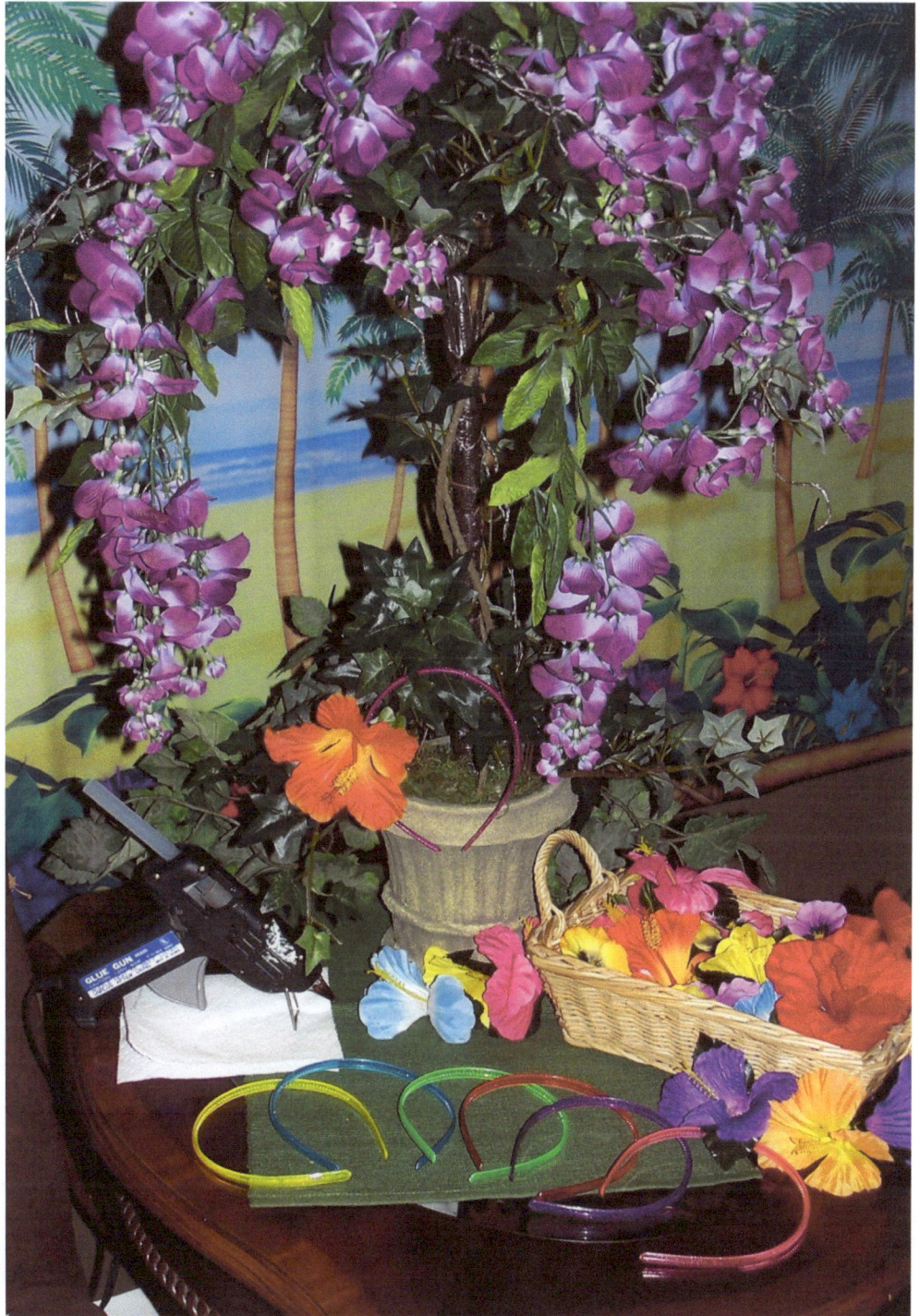

3. Floral Leis

Materials needed:

- Silk flowers, pulled off the stem. Place in wide flat baskets, (Flowers will have a hole in the middle from stem).
- Silk leaves, pulled off the stem, add to flower basket.
- Straws cut into 1" pieces. Place into several containers, (neon colored straws are most popular).
- Strands of natural polished hemp long enough to wear around the neck.

Have the children take a piece of hemp and thread on a flower petal or leaf followed by a piece of straw, and push to the far end. Continue interchanging until the strand is full. When finished tie the ends together.

Natural Polished Hemp
Chanvre naturel poli
CÁÑAMO NATURAL BRILLADO
133.3YDS / 121.9M   61266

Put straw pieces into coconut bowls.

Lay out scissors, hemp, and elastic string.

4. Floral Wrist and Ankle Bracelets

Cut thin elastic to fit around wrist and/or ankle without pulling too hard. Have the children thread the flowers and straws onto the elastic string and tie. They should go on and come off easily.

Tropical Magnetic Photo Frame

Lay a beach mat across the table for a tablecloth. Palm leaves arranged with a flower lei makes a striking centerpiece. Place tropical flowers around lei.

Materials needed:

- Colored foam sheets or foam frame kit (craft stores sell frames ready-cut in a kit with magnets).
- Foam luau shapes (self-adhesive)
- Thin washable markers
- Colored glitter/glitter glue
- Stickers (flowers, surf boards, sunsets, hula girl etc.)
- Self-adhesive magnet

Cut foam using the frame pattern on page 62, one per child. Stick magnet to the back of the frame. Set a frame in front of every chair. Lay out craft materials around the table as shown. Set children free to fashion their own creation. Write guest's name on his/her frame.

Take a picture of each child during the party.
Enclose the picture in a thank you card to be mailed later.
Inform the children that they will receive a picture in the mail to place in their frame.
This will become a treasured memento of the party.

Tropical Paddleball Craft

Materials needed:

- One paddleball paddle per child with
  tropical design to color, (sold at Oriental Trading Co.).
- Thin markers

Set a paddle in front of each chair. Lay markers of various colors around the table. Children color paddles. Set aside to take home or allow them to play when finished.

Paddleball paddles come sold in sets.

Tiki Tattoo Station

Materials needed:

- Table with grass skirt around it.
- Several removable tropic tattoos
- Bowl of water
- Clean wash cloths
- Tiki Tattoo Signs

Set out a table/card table with a grass skirt around the outside. Or build your own tiki hut, directions on page 11.

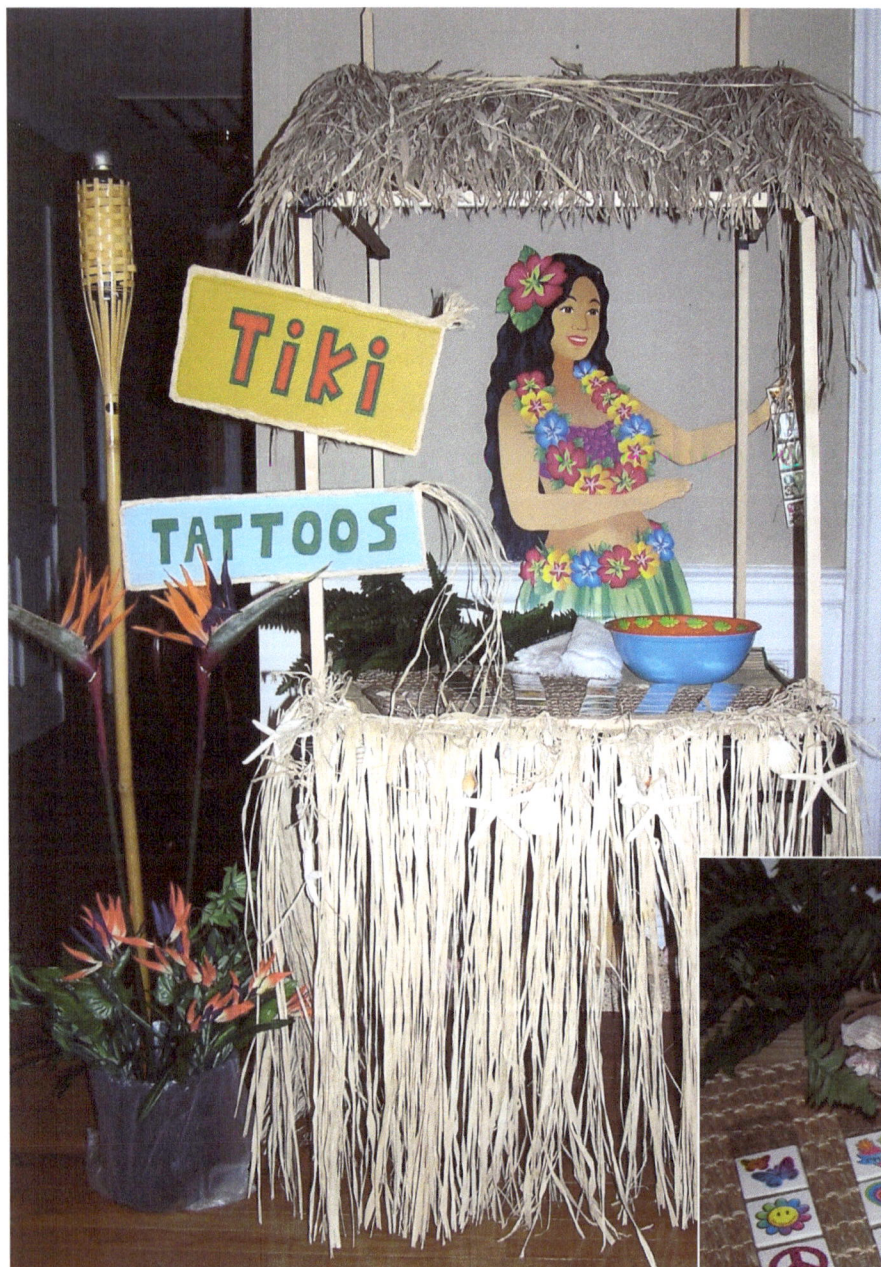

Spread out a variety of removable tattoos on the table for children to choose from. Have extras on hand for those who want more than one, but do set a limit.

Appoint someone to apply tattoos by wetting the wash cloth and applying pressure on the tattoo.

Some tattoos are rub-ons. Be familiar with how to apply before the party starts.

Tiki hut can later be used as a snack.

Tiny Bubbles, Floating in the Air

Materials needed:

- Bubble wands of various shapes and sizes
- Large bottle of bubble soap
- Bubble machine, optional

Choose an outdoor area and lay out wands on a grass mat or towel. Pour bubble soap into several bowls or pie tins and let children play freely. Another option is to purchase a bubble machine from a party or department store. Have the machine running while the children blow bubbles. Children enjoy chasing and popping bubbles floating in the air as much as making their own.

Tip: Have "Tiny Bubbles" by Hawaiian singer, Don Ho playing in the background. Check the internet for a download.

How to Open a Coconut

In selecting a coconut choose one that feels heavy. Shake and listen. You should hear the milk stirring inside. Check for three eyes at the smaller end of the coconut, (the eyes are small black circles). The shell should be intact without damage.

Step 1. Twist a corkscrew, or hammer a nail into the eye to make a hole. Hold the coconut over a bowl, and let the juice drain out the hole.

Step 2. Crack the shell open by hitting the edge of the coconut with the blunt side of a heavy knife or hammer. Give children the chance to see the inside.

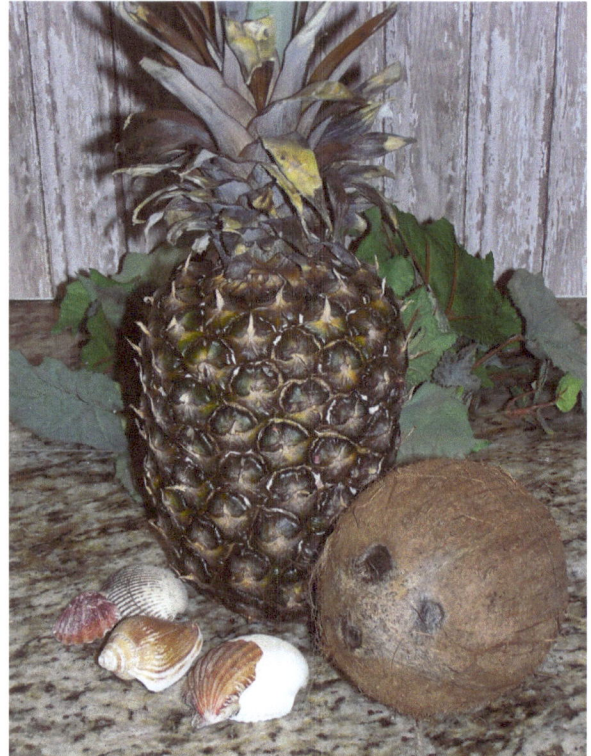

The taste of the coconut is foreign for most children. Have a bag of shredded coconut, or fun size coconut candy bars for the children to taste.

Step 1.

Step 2.

How to Cut & Eat a Pineapple

Step 1

Step 2

Step 3 & 4

Just a few easy steps to enjoy this delicious tropical fruit.

Step 1. Cut off crown (top) of pineapple.

Step 2. Cut fruit in half.

Step 3. Cut halves into quarters.

Step 4. Cut out core.

Step 5. Slice into wedges, place on tray or plate and serve.

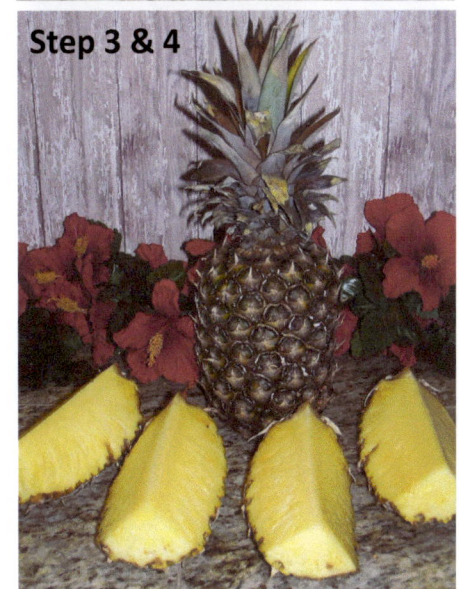

Party Menus

Tip: The key to making a kid's menu is to keep things simple. Many children do not like spicy foods. Some may not like pineapple, so use sparingly and have alternative fruit selections available. Do most of the cooking the night before.

Hawaiian Fried Rice

- 2 tablespoons butter
- 3 eggs
- 3 cups of rice (cooked)
- 1 cup of chopped carrots and peas (cooked)
- 3 tablespoon soy sauce
- salt and pepper to taste

Melt butter in large skillet. Add beaten eggs and keep stirring while cooking. Scramble eggs into small pieces. In a separate bowl add the remaining ingred. along with the eggs. Mix well. Return to skillet. Cook an additional 10-15 minutes.

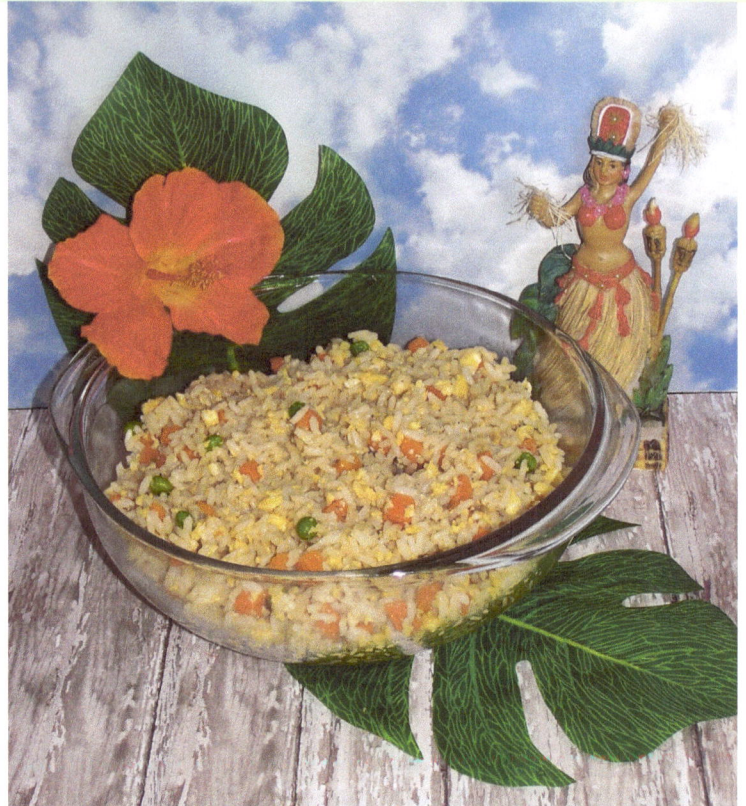

Teriyaki Fried Rice

The easiest way to make this dish is to purchase a package of chicken Teriyaki flavored rice. Cook as directed. Serve when ready. Garnish with sliced pineapple.

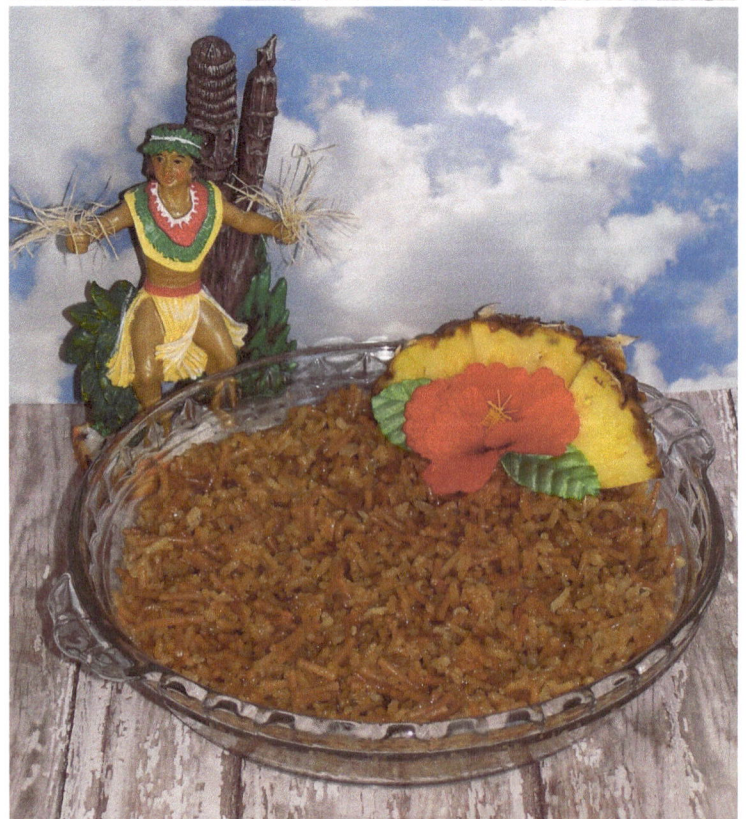

Tropical Fruit Ambrosia Salad

- 1 can (29 oz) tropical fruit salad (juice and all)
- 1 can (20 oz) crushed pineapple (juice and all)
- 1 can (11 oz) mandarin oranges (drained)
- 1 box (3.4 oz) instant vanilla pudding
- 1 box (3.4 oz) instant coconut cream pudding
- 1 1/2 cups colored miniature marshmallows
- 1 pint of Cool whip

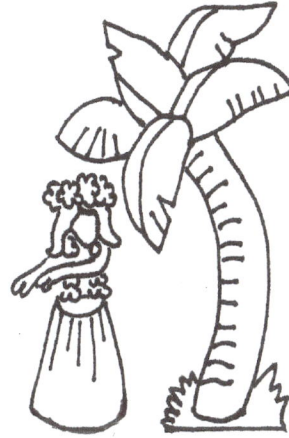

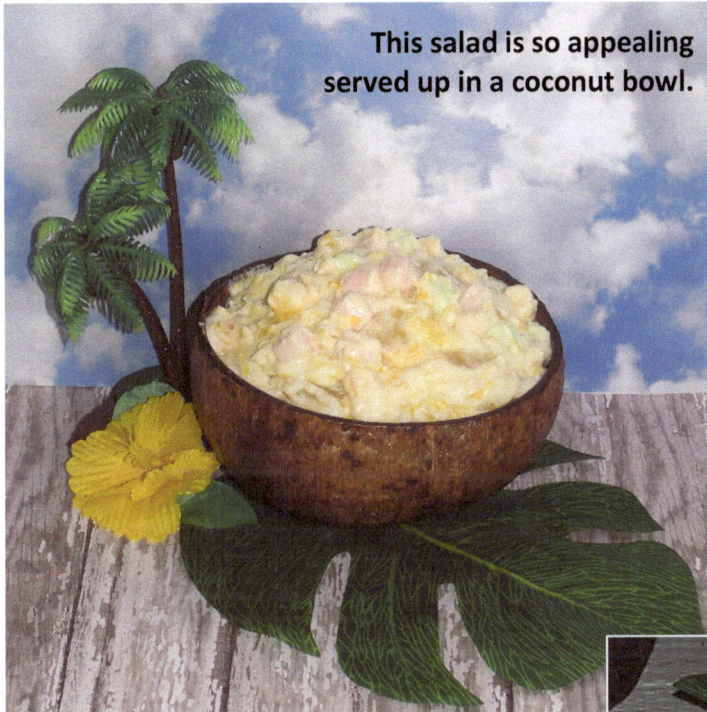

This salad is so appealing served up in a coconut bowl.

Combine first three ingredients into a large bowl; sprinkle instant pudding over fruits and stir. Add miniature marshmallows and cool whip.

Stir well and refrigerate. Make the night before for best results.

Give children a chance to experience the tropics by having a tray of tropical fruit to taste. The papaya fruit does not have a strong flavor. Cut into small slices for children to sample.

Cut up watermelon into slices and arrange on plate. Serve chilled.

Volcanic Potatoes with Melted Butter

- 1 bag of potatoes
- milk
- sour cream (optional)
- butter
- paprika

Pour water into a large pot and bring to a boil. Peel the potatoes and cut into pieces to cook faster. When water boils carefully place potatoes in water. Turn heat down to low and cook until a fork pokes easily through the potatoes. Use a colander to drain water and place into large mixing bowl. Using a potato masher utensil, crush the potatoes before you whip them with the mixer (The secret of creamy mashed potatoes). Add a little bit of milk, sour cream and butter. Mix. Be careful not to add too much milk or potatoes will be runny. Add a little at a time until you get the consistency you want. Preheat oven to 350 degrees. On a greased cookie sheet drop two large spoonfuls of mashed potatoes into several piles around the sheet. Using your hands, form the potatoes to look like volcanoes and poke a good size hole in the middle.

Sprinkle paprika on top and bake for 15-20 min. They will turn a little brown on the bottom.

When ready to serve melt butter and pour into the center of each volcano.

This can be done the night before and reheated in the oven.

Baked Ham with Pineapple

- 1 fully cooked bone-in ham (6-8 pounds)
- whole cloves
- 1/2 cup packed brown sugar
- 1/4 cup pineapple juice
- 1 can (8 oz) sliced pineapple
- maraschino cherries

Place ham in a roasting pan. Score the surface with shallow diagonal cuts, to form diamond shapes. Press whole cloves into the cuts. Cover with tin foil and bake for 1 1/2 hours at 325 degrees. Combine brown sugar and pineapple juice in bowl and spoon over the top of ham. Arrange pineapple slices on top of ham with cherries in the middle of each circle. Bake uncovered an additional 30-45 min. Meat thermometer should read 140 degrees. Let cool before carving.

Hawaiian Bread/Rolls

Hawaiian sweet bread can be found at your local grocery store. This makes a great addition to your meal. Rolls are popular with the young set so have extras on hand.

Blue Lagoon Fruit Waterfall

This is not as hard as it looks. Follow the steps and don't worry if your fruit tray is different. Make it your own personal edible creation.

It's exciting and fun to build this gorgeous centerpiece. Guests loved it!

Step 1. On a large tray or platter arrange foil-covered Styrofoam blocks as shown. Secure with wooden dowels. Place pineapple crown on top and place hollowed out bottom further down. Secure with a dowel.

Step 2. In a cascading line secure large clusters of purple grapes with toothpicks.

Step 3. Use green grapes to frame the purple. Arrange orange slices, cut in half using toothpicks. Add pineapple wedges.

Step 4. Fill in the centerpiece with strawberries and cantaloupe. The cantaloupe should be cut up into squares with a few wedges for adornment. Cover any toothpicks that show with a berry or grape.

Step 5. Place tropical hibiscus flower picks around the cascading fruit. Fill empty spots with fruit. When ready to serve fill pineapple bowl with vanilla yogurt.

Step 6. Tape tropical leaves to both sides of Styrofoam and surround with fruit. Secure all the fruit with toothpicks pressed into the foam. When finished check for toothpicks showing and cover with fruit. Refrigerate if possible. Use the fruit tray as a centerpiece for buffet table.

Dessert Recipes

Bali Banana Cheesecake

- 1 package cream cheese
- 3/4 cup sugar
- 1 teaspoon vanilla
- 2 eggs
- vanilla wafers
- 1 box (3.4 oz) instant banana cream pudding
- whipped cream (optional)
- cut banana slices for garnish

Cream the cheese at room temperature. Mix in sugar, vanilla and eggs. Beat until creamy. Put a vanilla wafer in each foil baking cup. Add mixture 2/3 full in each baking cup covering the wafer. Bake at 375 degrees 12-15 minutes. Do not over bake. Let cool and later refrigerate, (cheesecake will sink a little when cooled). Mix pudding according to package directions and refrigerate. The morning of party, spoon pudding on top of cheesecakes. Add a dollop of whipped cream. Keep refrigerated. When ready to serve garnish with a sliced banana on top.

Makes 1 dozen

Watermelon Mousse Parfaits

- 1/4 cup sugar
- 2 1/2 tablespoon cornstarch
- 1 large egg
- 1 1/2 cups low fat milk
- 25 watermelon hard candies crushed (Jolly Ranchers candy)
- 1 teaspoon watermelon syrup/flavoring
- red food coloring
- 2 cups whipped topping
- 4 boxes (3 oz) watermelon jell-o
- 9 oz clear plastic cups

Bottom layer:

Prepare 2 boxes of jell-o as directed and pour 2-3 tablespoons in 12 cups. Refrigerate until set.

Middle layer:

For mousse, whisk sugar, cornstarch, and egg in a medium sauce pan. Slowly whisk in milk, then watermelon candies, syrup flavoring with a few drops of red food coloring to look like watermelon. Bring to boil while gently whisking the bottom of pan to prevent the candy from sticking. Boil two minutes. Pour into medium bowl, lay plastic wrap directly over surface of mousse. Refrigerate 1 hour until cold. Remove plastic and fold in whipped topping. When jell-o has set, spoon 2-3 tablespoons of mousse on top of jell-o and spread leaving no holes.

Makes 1 dozen

Top layer:

Prepare last 2 boxes of jell-o as directed. Cool a bit, then spoon 2-3 tablespoons in each cup on top of mousse. Refrigerate until jell-o sets. When ready to serve, spoon a dollop of mousse on top. Garnish with candy.

Hawaiian White Chocolate Coconut Macadamia Cookies

- 2 1/2 cups flour
- 1 teaspoon baking soda
- 1/2 teaspoon salt
- 1 cup butter
- 2/3 cup sugar
- 2/3 firmly packed brown sugar
- 1 large egg (room temperature)
- 2 tablespoons milk
- 1 1/2 teaspoons of vanilla extract
- 1 cup white chocolate chips
- 1 cup shredded coconut
- 1 cup chopped macadamia nuts

Preheat oven to 350 degrees. Combine the first three ingredients in a large bowl and set aside. In a mixing bowl cream the butter and sugars until smooth. Add the egg, milk, and vanilla extract. Beat until creamy. Slowly add in the dry ingredients from the other bowl. Once batter is mixed, stir in the chips, coconut, and nuts. Drop cookies onto an ungreased cookie sheet, leaving a few inches between each cookie. Bake for 10-12 minutes or until lightly brown. Let cool for a few minutes before moving to rack.

Makes 3 dozen

Polynesian Coconut Cheesecake

Crust

- 1/2 cup butter (melted)
- 1 1/4 cups graham cracker crumbs
- 1/4 cups sugar

Filling

- 4 (8 oz) packages cream cheese (room temperature)
- 1 cup sugar
- 5 large eggs (room temperature)
- 1 1/2 cups of sweetened shredded coconut
- 2 tablespoons heavy cream
- 2 tablespoons vanilla extract
- 1 teaspoon coconut extract

Preheat oven to 325 degrees.

Hint: Place graham crackers into a zip lock bag and close. Roll over bag with a rolling pin to make crumbs for crust.

For crust: In a small bowl mix the graham cracker crumbs, sugar, and melted butter. Press into the bottom of a greased 10-inch spring pan. Bake for ten minutes. Remove from the oven and allow to cool in the pan.

Tip: Cream cheese at room temperature, it creams better with fewer lumps.

For Filling: Use a large bowl and beat the cream cheese on low speed until creamy and smooth. Gradually add the sugar and eggs, one at a time. Avoid lumps by stopping the mixer and scrape the sides of the bowl down with a spoon. Stir in the coconut, heavy cream, vanilla, and coconut extract. Pour batter into pan over the crust.

Bake until the edges are set and the center moves only a little when moving the pan. Be careful not to have the top crack from over cooking. Cooking time is 50 to 60 minutes. When finished turn off the oven and leave the oven door open ajar, letting the cheesecake cool for an additional hour inside oven. Cover and refrigerate for at least 12 hours. Garnish with dollops of whipped cream and shredded coconut. Tropical flowers add a nice touch. Spread additional flowers around the cake to give it that Polynesian Island flair.

Note: Don't panic if the cheesecake does crack in the middle. Turn off oven and let cool as directed. When ready to serve use the cool whip to fill in the cracks. The dessert will still taste wonderful.

Refrigerate until ready to serve.

Mandarin Orange Ice Cream Cake

- 1 box white cake mix
- 1 quart orange sherbet
- 2 (11 oz) cans of mandarin oranges
- 1 pint cool whip
- orange slices for decoration
- mint leaves for decoration

Prepare cake mix as directed. Pour into loaf pan and bake. Allow cake to cool for 15 minutes then place on wire rack. Clean cake pan and set aside. Place scoops of sherbet in a blender and mix while adding mandarin orange slices from one can. The sherbet should be smooth. Line loaf pan with saran wrap. This will be used to lift the sherbet out of the pan. Spoon sherbet into loaf pan and spread evenly. Place in the freezer to harden.

When cake has cooled turn the cake onto its side and cut down the center. Once sherbet has frozen, take off the top half of the cake. Gently pull sherbet out of the pan and place on top of cake bottom. Place cake top over sherbet. Cover and place in freezer.

Day of party, frost cake with whipped cream. Decorate with mandarin oranges (dab excess juice off mandarin slices with a paper towel before placing on cake) and mint leaves. Place in freezer until ready to serve.

Beverages

Banana Punch

- 7 cups of water
- 1/2 cup sugar
- 5 bananas mashed
- 1 can (6 oz) frozen orange juice
- 1 can (6 oz) frozen lemonade
- 1 can (46 oz) pineapple juice
- 1 quart of ginger ale

Boil water and sugar for 5 minutes, cool and add the remaining ingredients except the ginger ale. Freeze until solid. Remove from freezer two to three hours before serving.

When ready to serve, pour the slushy punch into punch bowl and add ginger ale.

Float decorative plastic ice cubes or sliced fruit on top.

Arrange cups around punch bowl. Guests may serve themselves.

Refrigerate unused punch for later use.

Sea shell punch bowls are available for purchase in many local party stores.

Tropical Fruit Smoothies

Note: Because the fruit is frozen the drink will be slushy without having to add ice or ice cream. Drinks may be a little thick at first but will thin out shortly, Add juice if mixture is too thick for the blender. Serve with a tiny umbrella or pieces of fruit. Use plastic margarita or daiquiri glasses for fun!

Strawberry Banana Smoothie

- 2 peeled frozen bananas
- 2 cups of frozen strawberries
- 3 cups of refrigerated apple juice

Place all three ingredients in a blender. Mix well until smooth. Pour into cups and serve.

Tropical Smoothie

- 2 peeled frozen bananas
- 2 cups of canned tropical frozen fruit
- 3 cups of refrigerated apple juice

Place all three ingredients in a blender. Mix well until smooth. Pour into cups and serve.

Party Games

Limbo

You will need a bamboo stick or pole and a person to hold each end. Start off with the pole about shoulder height. Each child is to walk slowly underneath the pole holding their heads back and looking up at the pole. Touching the pole is not allowed.

After everyone has had a turn, lower the pole. Children may need to bend their knees and arch their backs as the pole is lowered. If a child touches the pole or ground or falls down, they are out of the game. The last one under the pole wins the game.

Bora Bora Butt Blast

Divide children into two teams. Each team member is given a balloon. Blow up all the balloons prior to the party and store in a large garbage bag. Always blow up more balloons than you think you will need!

Lay down a bamboo stick or pole (broomstick works) to make a start line. Set two chairs several feet from the starting line and cover with a beach towel.

On the word "Go" the first person from each team takes a balloon and hits it in the air punching it toward the chairs. Arriving at the chair, they place the balloon in the chair and pop it by sitting on it.

Once the balloon has popped, the player runs back to his/her team and tags the next person who repeats the same action. The team that finishes first wins the game.

Hidden Shells in the Sand

Before the party fill a baby pool (line pool first with plastic) or sandbox with sand and hide lots of small sea shells in the sand. Each child, one at a time, is blindfolded and given one minute to find as many shells as they can. Players who want to keep their shells, may place them together with his/her take home favors. The one who finds the most shells wins.

Musical Beach Towels

This game is played like musical chairs, but using towels instead. Fold towels in half and lay out in a circle on grass or deck. Have one less towel than the number of players. Have each one hula to Hawaiian music around the outside of the towels, facing inward. When the music stops each player will sit on a towel. The one who has no towel to sit on is out and moves to the sideline. One towel is then picked up and the game begins again. Last one sitting on a towel wins.

Pass the Coconut

This game is a version of wonder ball, but with a twist. You may get to eat the coconut and drink the milk inside after the game is over.

However, if you prefer, purchase a fake one used for drinks at a party store. Seat the players in a circle and give one player the coconut to begin the game by tossing it to his/her left. As the coconut is passed around the circle, everyone sings the following poem in a sing-song manner.

"The coconut goes round and round, to catch it quickly you are bound. If you are caught with it at last, then you-are-out."

The one left holding the coconut at the end of the verse is eliminated and must leave the circle. The game continues until there is one person left in the circle holding the coconut. He/she is pronounced the winner. If a real coconut is used in the game, you might want to follow the simple steps on how to open a coconut on page# 34.

Hula Hoops

You can have lots of fun with hula hoops. Here's some games and contests that will keep your guests laughing while promoting team spirit. Play fast moving Hawaiian or Beach Boys songs during hula games to keep the momentum going.

Lead the spectators in cheering for each challenger!

1. **Hula Endurance** - Hold three or four competitions to test staying power. All contestants swing hula hoops at the same time. The challenge is to keep those hoops up and twirling the longest.

2. **Hula Strength and Agility** - Have contestants one at a time take three or four hoops, and using their neck, waist, and arms, keep all the hoops going for 30 seconds.

3. **Hula Relay Race** - Set up two lines of 3 to 4 cones with at least five feet between each cone. Divide children into two teams and line up for the relay. Each team is given a hula hoop. On the signal "Go" the first person from each line hula zig-zags in and around each cone, up and back. Once back to the start line the next one takes the hoop and repeats the same task. The first team to have everyone hula up and back wins.

4. **Jumping Through Hoops Race** - Players line up at the start line. Mark a finish line several feet/yards ahead. Each child has a hoop. At the word "Go" children pick up his/her hoop, jump through, lay it on the ground and turn around two times inside the hoop and jump out. Repeat this sequence while moving forward to the finish line. First person to cross the finish line wins.

5. **Passing the Hoop** - Divide youngsters into two teams and have them line up, facing each other, side by side, in a row holding hands. On the word "Go" the first person from each team picks up a hula hoop and passes through without letting go of his neighbor's hand. The hoop is passed along to the next person. This continues until the hoop reaches the end. The last one in line passes through the hoop and places it on the ground announcing his/her team as winner.

6. **Hoop a Hula Girl** - Everyone breaks up into teams of two. One person throws, the other one catches. Place one hula hoop on the ground for the thrower to stand in. Place a second hula hoop several feet in front for the catcher to stand in (closer for younger children). Working one team at a time, the thrower stands in one hoop while the catcher stands in other hoop. Five hoops are handed to the thrower to toss. When each team has had a turn, reverse the players. Throwers become catchers and catchers become throwers.

The object of the game is to catch as many hoops as possible without moving out of the circle.

Use any body part: arms. legs, head or foot, but no hands.

When each team has had a turn, reverse the players.

Throwers become catchers and catchers become throwers.

Spear throwing game using a bamboo spear. Directions on page 64.

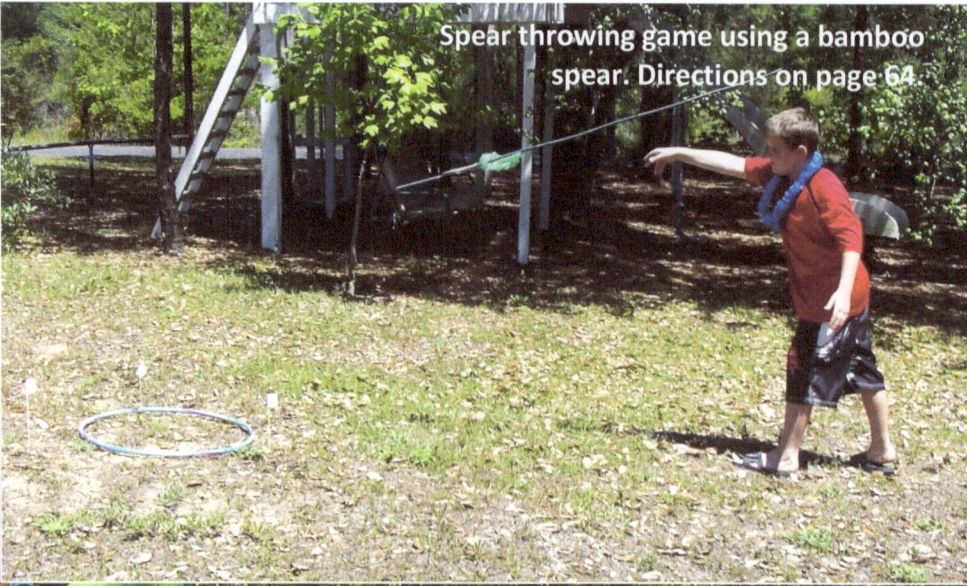

The rolling stones game requires skill and patience. Play on a hard surface for better rock rolling.

Traditional Ancient Hawaiian Games

While having fun with friends, Island warriors often show off their prowess competing in feats that test strength, agility, and endurance. Below are several contests Hawaiians enter into during luau festivities.

Spear Throwing - This game is to test which warrior can toss a spear or dart and hit a target.

Lay a hula hoop on the ground and mark the bull's eye center. One at a time each contender is given a spear and made to stand several feet away from the target. He/she has one try to hit the middle bull's eye in the hula hoop. Use wooden skewers taped with player's name to mark the spot where his/her spear landed. The competitor who comes the closest to the bull's eye, is declared the winner.

Rolling Stones - Set up a cardboard palm tree against a tree or wall. One at a time, each participator is given a small round stone to roll or toss toward the tree. Mark the spot where the stone lands and give the stone to the next rival for a turn. Make sure everyone understands that the object of the game is not to hit the tree, but to land the stone as close as they can. Whoever lands his/her stone the closest wins.

Foot Races - Hawaiians hold foot races to find the swiftest runner. Set up a starting and finishing post and have players line up. At the signal, players run for the goal line.

Hold a three-legged race. Team up players by two's. Tie the left leg of one player to the right leg of another player. At the signal all contestants run for the finish line on their "three" legs. Use discretion: this is an age appropriate game.

After the games are over, hold a medal awards ceremony Olympic style. Award the winners of each game with a lei.

Learning to Hula Dance

The hula dance is an ancient tradition of Hawaii, gracefully performed by Hawaiian dancers using hands and body movements to tell a story. Below are some hula steps to practice while hula music plays in the background.

Basic Hula Steps

❖ **Ami** - Rotate hips to the right going counterclockwise. Rotate hips to the left going clockwise.

❖ **Hela** - Point right foot out front and bring it back. Point left foot out front and bring it back.

❖ **Huli** - Circle around while swaying hips.

❖ **Kaholo** - Slide step forward, side step back, and slide step to the right side, and slide step to the left.

❖ **Ka'o** - Sway hips by shifting weight from the right side to the left side.

❖ **Leie** - Step right and bring feet together, shift weight. Step left and bring feet together, shift weight. Action can be done moving forward or backward.

❖ **Ocean Hand Movement** - Hands gently wave from right to left imitating the rhythmic movement of ocean waves.

❖ **Love Hand Movement** - Hands cross against the chest.

❖ **Tide Roll Hand Movement** - Hands repeatedly roll one over the other like the rise and fall of the sea.

❖ **Swaying Palms Hand Movement** - Raise left arm and bend to cross in front of the chest with the palm down to represent the land. Place right elbow with arm standing upright at a 45 degree angle on the left arm to represent a tree. Sway fingers like palm fronds waving in the breeze.

❖ **Rainbow Hand Movement** - Palms of both hands meet at the left side. The right hand lifts and circles to the right to form the shape of a rainbow.

❖ **Rising Sun Hand Movement** - Bring hands to the knees, then slowly raise both hands to rise above the head using the arms to form the sun.

❖ **Swirling Winds Hand Movement** - The left hand extends forward while the right hand circles overhead twice.

❖ **Singing/Story Hand Movement** - Gracefully bring right hand to the mouth to signify a song.

❖ **End of Dance Movement** - Stretch both hands straight out in front, one on top of the other, palms facing the ground, and bow head.

Pattern Page

Flower Pattern for lei invitations

Flamingo pattern

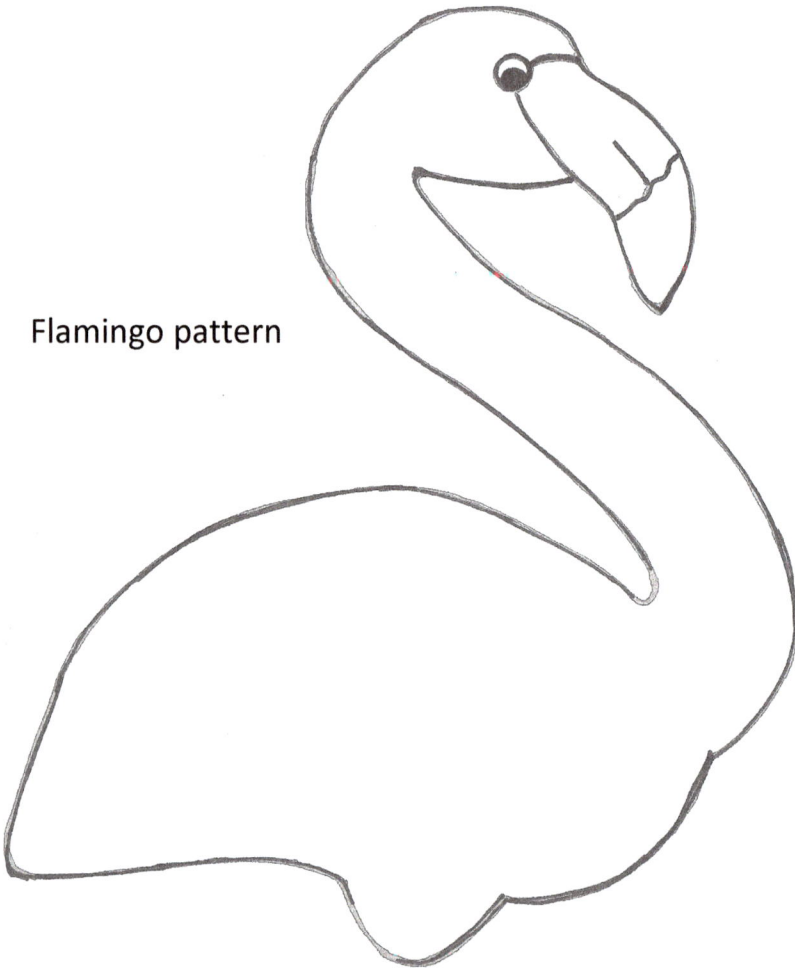

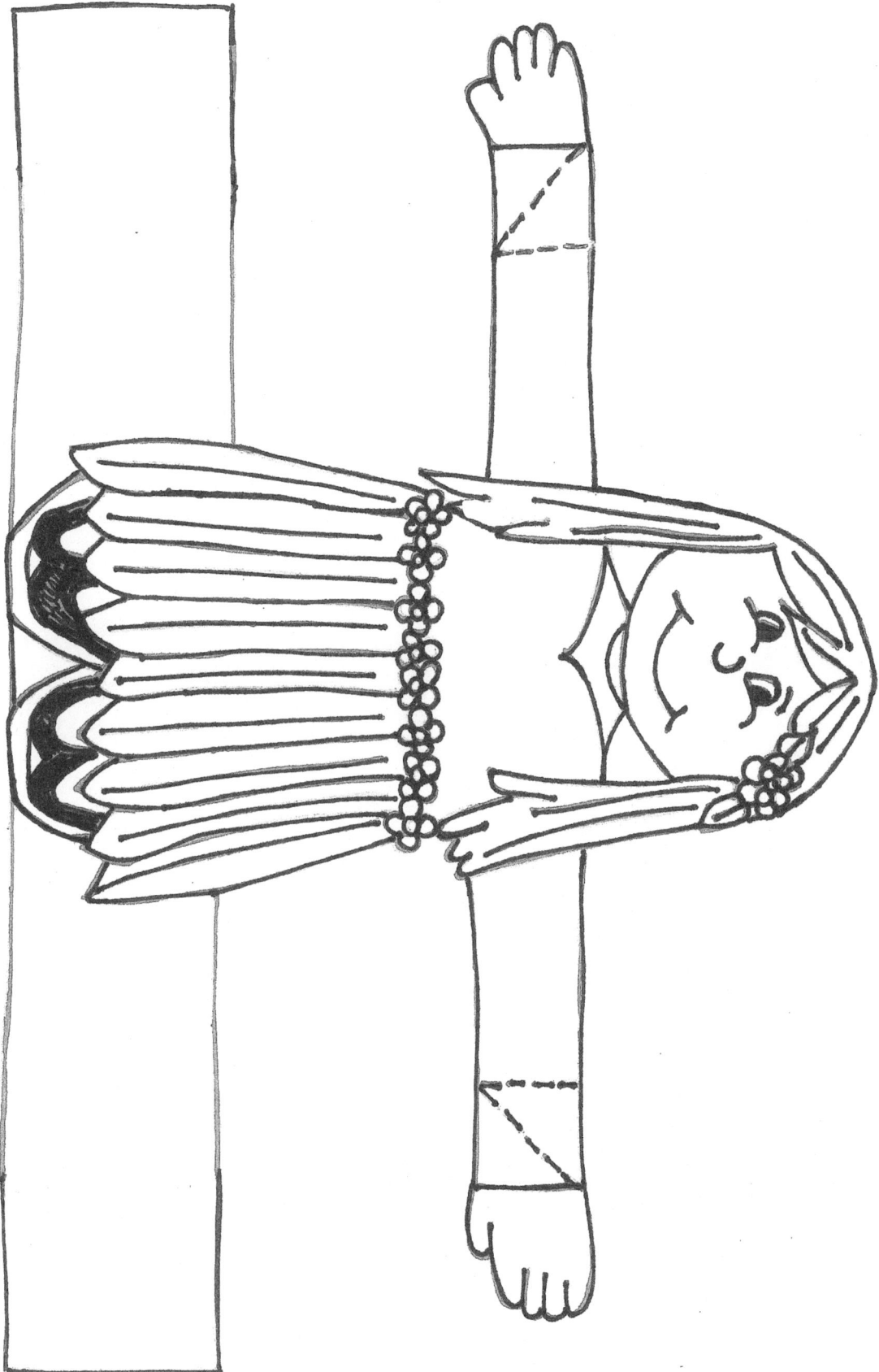

Photo Frame Pattern

Party Favor and Prize Suggestions

- Floral leis made earlier along with those given upon arrival
- Plastic coconut or pineapple drink cups
- Magnetic photo frames
- Decorated paddleball
- Headbands, wrist, and ankle bracelets
- Grass skirts decorated with sea shells
- Small baggie of colorful sea shells or star fish
- Hula dolls
- Colorful tropical fans
- Coconut candy bars
- Bottles of bubbles

Directions and Party Tips

Directions for Spear:

Materials needed:

- Metal skewer
- Bamboo pole
- Packing, duck, or electrical tape

Use tape to attach the metal skewer to the top of the bamboo pole. Start wrapping tape around the bottom of skewer working your way toward the top. Stop half way. Tie or wrap lei around the tape. You will only need one spear for the games. It is not meant to be a toy to play with. **Be careful of accidents!**

Directions for Tissue Flowers:

Materials needed:
- Tissue paper sheets 25x20" in a variety of bright colors
- Pipe cleaners

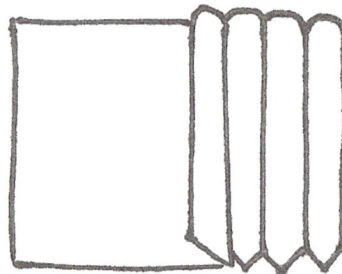

Lay out at least five tissue sheets of the same color, one on top of another. Starting at the bottom, fold the sheets into accordion pleats all the way to the top. Hold the folded tissue paper in the middle and wrap the end of a pipe cleaner around the center. Pull out the tissue paper one at a time forming a flower as you go. The pipe cleaner serves as fastener and stem.

Party Tips:

1. Garage sales and thrift stores are the best place to find props for a party. Sometimes you can pick up some really low-cost party items.

2. Do all the decorations and most of the cooking the day before the party. Enjoy the fun instead of working to finish last minute tasks.

3. Choose the activities that best suit your child and his/her guests. Children should have fun without frustration or embarrassment.

4. The best parties our family enjoyed were those in which we all worked together to make it a success. Have the children color the invitations and set up table activities. Things do not always have to be perfect! Helping gives children a feeling of ownership and pride knowing they have a hand in making the party a success.

5. Don't be afraid to over invite. Several guests will not be able to attend. Call two days before the party date to get the final number count of guests.

6. Artificial flowers work great for a young people's party, especially if you're on a budget. Most of my flowers were bought for a dollar or less. For an adult party always use real flowers.

7. Cardboard is wonderful for craft work. Wholesale or appliance stores are known to have boxes. Call ahead of time so some can be set aside for you to pick up. Cardboard can be sewn together using a large needle and fishing line. This works better than tape for attaching objects. The signs and tiki hut roof were sewn together using fishing line.

8. Don't sweat the small stuff . . . have fun and enjoy this time together with your child/children! Create wonderful memories to last a life-time.

About the Author

Author, Robin Gillette has dedicated more than twenty years working with pre-school and elementary kids, at-risk teens, and disabled children. Using her BS in Human Development and Family Relations, she has developed and implemented learning programs and activities for hundreds of children. She has also conducted training courses to instruct and motivate volunteer teachers in the areas of child development, teacher/child relationships, learning centers, social skills, and self esteem improvement.

Interaction with her own son and daughter, as well as young students, has presented Robin with ample opportunities to set up parties and activities relating to a variety of themes and events. She has now transformed her love for creating children's parties into her own unique party creation business to help parents and teachers design and successfully implement parties using the same techniques, food and game ideas that Robin has used for over 20 years.

The author's website, "letspartyhereshow.com" dedicated to the "Let's Party, Here's How" book series, covers a wide variety of party theme books. Each theme book comes complete with all the tools needed to make a successful party for young and old alike. Instructional videos and links to supplies are also included. So, if you like to party and want to learn how, visit www.letspartyhereshow.com.

Party Notes and Comments